T0198035

girl made of glass

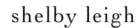

shelby leigh

central
avenue
PUBLISHING

2023

Published by Central Avenue Publishing, an imprint of Central Avenue Marketing Ltd.
www.centralavenuepublishing.com

GIRL MADE OF GLASS

Trade Paperback: 978-1-77168-276-3
Epub: 978-1-77168-277-0

Published in Canada
Printed in United States of America

1. POETRY / Women Authors   2. POETRY / General

10 9 8 7 6 5 4 3 2 1

to the girls made of glass:
you will not always want to shatter

contents

the nightmares

past selves and the moments that haunt us

i used to be afraid of the dark.
every night, i found shadows in the sinking sun
and heard breaths beneath the bed
and creaks in the closet.
as i got older and the fear faded,
i realized i'd created these monsters
to feel less alone.
because when i'm alone, i'm left
with my own thoughts.

no moving shadows on the walls
to distract from the
horrors that haunt my head.

i hold fear
like i'm holding someone's hand.
i've grown too comfortable with the feeling.
i don't want to let go
and be alone.

fear lives with me—
it stands in the mirror,
crawls into bed,
and hovers over my head at night.
it knows i won't sleep
with its eyes piercing my mind.

i am held tightly in its grasp.

when i am anxious, i imagine yarn at my feet.
my stomach has knots and so does my throat—
my entire body. they are intricately woven,
spinning around my skull like spools
of yarn, squeezing my brain and making my
head throb, cutting the circulation around
my wrists. i pull my hair like i'm a puppet,
try to unravel and spill free.

i imagine the yarn pooling at my feet.
i imagine the things i could make if i were free.
i imagine a world where i am not tied to
overthinking, anxiety, trying to please everyone.
when i am anxious, i imagine yarn at
my feet, but the truth is

i don't know who i am
without these knots
tightening inside me.

I don't know who I am without these knots tightening inside me.

i'm afraid i will
never be loved as
much as i love.
i'm afraid of emptying
my soul into someone's
hands and watching them
drop it.

i'm afraid i'll never get it back.
i'm afraid i'll never be the same
person i was before they emptied me.

i take all my regrets,
secrets,
missed chances,
scoop them into my hands and
bury them beneath the wood floor.
i try to step over that spot in my kitchen
where the floorboards lift and
my past tries to escape.

sometimes i secretly hope it will escape,
haunt me again,
make me feel something again.
but until then i'll step over the floorboards,
creep around the creaks,
sit in this silence and
pretend my past
will not live in my future.

my lungs have forgotten how to
inhale slowly, exhale calmly.
breathe deeply and feel at peace.
my palms no longer remember
the feeling of a steady heartbeat
when i press them to my chest.
but my mind never lets go.
it remembers everything.

nights often end with
a swarm of thoughts
clouding my mind,
of the next day
and yesterday
and days i've left behind.

afraid to
fall asleep because
i don't want to lose
these moments i've held on to
like skeletons in the closet.
even the ones that break me.
because without them

i don't know
who i would be.

the bad memories sit heavy on my lungs
and i don't have the strength to push them off.

they make it harder to breathe,
but that's okay.

sometimes i feel like i don't deserve
to breathe easy.

how many
days
will pass
before
the memories
FADE?
(what if they
never do?)

at night
i think about all the times
i should have spoken up and
didn't.
the times
my lips tried
to form words but stayed closed.
my voice tried
a scream but barely reached a whisper.

my heart breaks just a little
every time i stay quiet,
but even then, my body
does not make
a sound.

no one can hear my pain.
not even me.

when the fear sets in,
i am home.
this fast-beating heart
is my default setting.

sadness shatters glass.
sadness bruises my knees,
bloodies my knuckles.

sadness holds me down
like a rope pulled taut over my ribs.

sadness pushes me underwater
and holds like an anchor.

sadness looms
like a storm cloud
every
single
day.

but sadness will never win.
i will never let it win.

please
promise
me
you'll never
let the
sadness
win.

i'm scared i'll never find the
rowdy, untroubled child i was.
the one without a care in the world.
she ran far into the forest and never came back.

i'm still running after her—
wading through streams and
climbing over fallen trees—

searching tirelessly for any
sign she still exists.

my hands have been carrying
around this heartache.
they are sore and tired,
weak from the weight.
i can't help but wonder
what it would feel like to drop it.
to empty my hands
and let my pain shatter
on the ground.

i feel so much lighter already.

comfort does not come easily to me.

it is

a slow drip in my veins,
a knot unraveling in my chest.

it is

days spent wondering when i will reach out
my hand and find yours is no longer there to hold.

it is

eyes searching in the night
and lungs pulling for air.

and when the comfort finally comes,
i spend my days wondering how soon
it will be gone.

i wonder if everyone's
life is the same:
sorrow sprinkled with
a little joy and a little pain.

i wonder if other people
have perfect days,
or just moments in time
when things are okay.

i wonder if other people
wish their sorrows away
and spend the happy moments
wondering if the sadness will stay.

perfect.
perfect.
perfect.
my thumbs scroll through
photo after photo of perfectly
edited and altered bodies.
my eyes are numb and blurry
but my mind is wide awake,
memorizing every detail so i can
look in the mirror later and
compare how different
i am from
who i want to be.

my biggest fear is leaving this earth
without achieving something great,
walking miles and miles but never
leaving a permanent footprint.

it happened again:
moments of doubt
turned the door handle quietly,
crept in softly.
i used to make room
for them in my head.
i'd shove the happy moments aside
and let the bad ones
take over
for days, weeks, months.

but
i am done
letting this doubt
run my body
like my life is a game
and someone else's hands
are on the controller.

i am taking back my fears.
folding up my doubts and insecurities.
tossing them in a dresser drawer
like clean laundry.

easy.

i won't trick my mind into thinking
they've gone,
that it's simple to cram away
the worries that plague me and
live life without them.

but every time the dresser
drawer creeps open
and the fears begin to unfurl,
i will practice folding
and folding
and folding
once more.

forgive yourself for the times
you've messed up.
forgive yourself for the times
you haven't been kind
to yourself or to others.
forgive yourself for the times
you've needed love and
didn't have any to give.

but don't forget.

forgetting won't change the mistakes you've made,
but remembering them will help you
become the person you're meant to be.

my past is a ghost that
floats behind me,
peering over my shoulder,
reminding me of where i've been
and how far i have to go.

my past tries to haunt me,
but really it gives me hope.
because when i look back,
i notice how different i am today—
it gives me the strength to keep

moving forward.

it's okay to regret mistakes you've made.
you'll learn from them and forgive
yourself one day.

it's okay to find happiness again.
one day, you'll realize you were
never really broken.

it's okay to fall to the floor.
but please, show yourself love
and rise once more.

some days i feel empty.
a hollow shell gliding through
life, floating.
and other days i feel full
of laughter and joy
and sunshine.
i never know which one
i'm going to be
when i start my day,
but at least i've opened my eyes.

the mirror

self-doubt and the girl made of glass

striking (verb):

some types of glass
change color when reheated.
some of the ruby family,
known for their deep, beautiful red,
are actually clear
until exposed to a flame.

each day, i learn of something
that is altered so it becomes
more beautiful, more desirable.
it is no wonder i have spent
so much time thinking up ways
to do the same to me.

i am the girl made of glass,
the girl who spends her days
imagining what it would be like to
rearrange her pieces
as if she were repairing
a broken mirror.

i turn my face
when i see my
reflection.
how can i learn
to love a
body
that shelters
me yet makes
me feel so
exposed?

reflections: i step in front of the mirror and my vision dims. i've never noticed how i squint my eyes when i see my reflection. i want to look away but my brain tells me no. keep looking, keep analyzing. i'm supposed to be writing down a few reasons why i love myself but honestly, i'd rather pull my own teeth with drugstore tweezers. *ha.* i think i'll write down that i love how i can make myself laugh. i think i'll step in front of the mirror tomorrow and try to keep my eyes open. i think i'll reach for my hairbrush or chapstick or those drugstore tweezers and try to fix something, anything. i can't remember the last time i said *i love you* to my reflection. i think i will tomorrow, but not today.

the mirror is deadly.
it takes its victims slowly.
it pulls us into the glass,
and we become one with
our reflections.
it holds our gaze and
tricks us into thinking
we are
not enough.
it tells us
not to look away

until we break.

the girl made of glass
taunts me.

when i frown,
she slowly smiles.

when i turn
to hide the parts of me

i don't wish to see,
she points them out to me.

the girl made of glass
bends down,
picks up the pieces of me
that have gathered around
our ankles,
and cements them to her skin.

she grows stronger
each and every time i
shatter.

i'm fragile in your hands,
but i'm the weakest in my own.
i don't know anyone who can
break me
like i
break me.

i've always been told one day
i'll find myself,
but i know exactly who i am.
i've spent years not wanting to be her.

how to be insecure:

1. place your hair in front of your face like a curtain.
2. don't laugh too loud. when you laugh, cover your mouth with your hand.
3. (but not for too long, or they'll see your chewed-up nails.)
4. blush when you hear someone laughing. they're probably laughing at you.
5. don't make eye contact. don't draw attention. don't raise your hand.
6. when you get home, think about everything you did. everything you said. everything you could have done differently.

i see her in my nightmares.
she never strays from sight,
even though i wish the fears
away with all my might.

she once stayed in the mirror.
now she lives in my head.
when i think she's disappeared,
she follows me to bed.

i'm scared she'll never vanish,
the girl that haunts my nights.
but i pray she'll begin to fade
if i learn to treat her right.

i've always hated looking at my hands
with their bitten nails and pale, blotchy skin.

but when you're shy, your hands become
your armor. your safety net.

a mask to hide your face when you're embarrassed.
an instrument to play to keep your nerves at bay.

i've always hated looking at my hands
but all along, they've been protecting me.

i'm still learning that my body
is not the enemy i've always
thought it to be.

when i am alone, i talk to myself
and it is dangerous.
i do not offer advice
or love or a hug.
i say
these problems don't matter.
i say
you brought this on yourself.
i say
you could have done better.

i can feel my body wanting.
it shivers when it's cold,
aches when it's hurt,
flutters when it's anxious.
but how does a body warn us
when it wants love?
does it break little by little?
does it ever reach a point
where it can't be saved?

(am i too late?)

if i were given the option
to either
repair my body—
fix everything that i think
is wrong—
or
repair my mind—
the years of self-doubt
that have consumed me—
i don't know which one
i would choose

and that terrifies me.

i wonder who i would be today
if i hadn't spent years trying so hard
to be someone else.

i don't think i've ever felt like i belong.
i have never walked into a roomful
of other people and
felt comfort wrap its arms around me.
i look for watching eyes and judging smiles
so i can confirm what my mind
always tells me:

you don't belong.

i don't think i've ever given myself
the chance to belong.
when i walk into a room
filled with people,
i look for the judgment.
i seek the doubt.
i'm used to being on the outside
so that is where i stay.
glued to the walls,
fingertips searching for chips in the paint.

where i belong.

i know exactly who i want to be.
i've shaped this ideal person in my head,
from the color she paints her nails in winter
to the silk pajamas she wears to bed.
i think about her when i mess up,
when things don't go my way.
how she would laugh away the stress
and know exactly what to say.
she is the version of me that i most want to be.
so happy and kind and always carefree.

i've tried so hard to be this perfect girl
that i've forgotten how to be me.

girl made of glass,
you see yourself from the outside,
but inside there is so much more.

girl made of glass,
you were created with compassion
and inspiration and light.

girl made of glass,
don't let the self-doubt
stop you from thriving in this life.

the shattering

relationships and the ones who try to break us

melting point (noun):

when glass reaches high temperatures,
it can liquify and bend.
it can mold to new shapes.
it can become something new.

you tried to find my melting point,
scorching me again and again
so you could mold me into
the girl you wanted.

and i helped
ignite the fire.

i didn't just bend over backwards for you.
i broke my bones. shattered my soul.
to you, it was love.
to me, it was anything but.

I don't know how to open UP without being let DOWN.

they say
it won't hurt forever
but i will never
experience forever.

so tell me,
how much longer
do i have to live
with this pain?

i don't like being alone,
and i know that's not a good enough reason
to hold on to you.
but i still can't let go.
because i hate half-empty beds
and i hate goodbyes
and i hate *we'll stay friends*
and i hate not knowing
if i'll see you again.

because i hate me for
not loving you anymore.

i read a lot of books and
watch a lot of movies about
strangers becoming lovers.
but what happens when
lovers become strangers?
when you don't recognize
the person you once told
everything to?

what happens when you
open your eyes one day
and the love is just

gone?

on crisp autumn days i walk outside,
leaves crunching beneath
the soles of my shoes.
some days i watch the ground
ahead and other days
i watch the trees
canopy over me,
slivers of blue sky bright
between the branches.
the wind comes
swiftly and easily,
knocking my body off-balance
and sweeping my hair around
like a halo.

it is confusing at first
to feel connected to the earth
and suddenly—disoriented.
that's how i think about you now.
a gust of wind that wanted
to be a tornado.
just a harmless, fleeting thing.
you tried to knock me to the ground
but my feet only stumbled.
i swept my hands through my hair
and i held my arms out for balance
and i kept walking,
leaves crunching beneath
the soles of my shoes.

a snowflake lands on my hand
and melts before i have the chance
to take in all of its beauty.

i notice my reflection
in the water droplets that rest
on my palm.

they vanish
before i have the chance
to take in all of my beauty.

our love bloomed in the spring,
grew stronger with the rainfall.
stayed steady in summer,
flourished in the heat.
our love was vibrant
in autumn, like the
leaves beneath our feet.
and when our love
died in winter—
when the first frost
buried our hearts in the cold—

i prayed for spring.

i am
still
praying
for
spring.

my hands are numb from the cold
and i can't stop thinking about how
you once wrapped your fingers around mine
and brought them back to life.

i can still taste the happiness
you spoon-fed me like fruit.
some days it sits like sugar
on my tongue, and other days
it closes up my lungs.

i am still learning to be happy
without you,
to feel valid and worthy
in my skin.
i never thought i would regret you,
but when i daydream about my happiness,

i wish i had never
let you in.

the scariest part
about giving your heart
to someone else is that
sometimes they leave
and forget to give it back.

sometimes you are left
clutching at your chest,
tearing through skin,
hoping for a heartbeat.

in every relationship i am
too much.
too much love to give.
too many feelings shared.
but i don't know how to close off
a heart
that needs love to feel alive.
i don't know how to hold myself back
from giving.
even if it leaves me

empty.

i am a giver.
giver of too many chances and
too much forgiveness.
too many *it's okay*'s
and not enough
you really hurt me's.

you feast on the
broken, empty parts of me.
and i fall for it
every time you tell me
you will make me
full again.

this longing for you never fades.
it eats away at my soul and
comes back for more.
this wanting is a monster.
this desire is a devil.
working tirelessly to ensure
i never think of anything but you.

i dream of you
even when i am awake
because i cannot bear
the thought of
you
leaving my head.

ode to your hands

i still search for them,
wish for them,
feel them,
need them.

when our love came to an end,
i welcomed a new beginning.
within me, i found an empty home
in which to pour all the love
i had been giving away.

i haven't heard your voice
in two years, and i think
i'm happier because of it.
missing you gets easier
when i can't remember
how
i love you
sounded
coming out of your mouth.

in september, i step outside my door
and see our love written in the clouds.
in december, i look out the window
and see your name in white on the ground.
in may, i feel free and whole
and i wonder if you've moved on too.
in august, i look to the sky once more
and see your name among the clear blue.

do we ever
truly move on
from

missing you is a funny thing.
sometimes i feel relieved
that you no longer
linger in my body.
and sometimes i feel saddened
that you no longer
take up space in my mind.

i am nostalgic for the days
when you lived there happily.

i am nostalgic for the days when we were *happy.*

the wrong love can shatter you.
the wrong love can chisel you down
into remnants of the person you were
before they ever
put their
hands on you.

the right love will help you rebuild.
the right love will help you search
for the missing pieces.

and when they find one—
a piece of you that
you'd tucked away to keep from
getting hurt again—
they'll place it in your palm,
wrap their fingers around yours.
they'll say,

keep it with you until you're ready.

we can learn a lot
from the love story of
the sun and the moon.
trading places day and night,
allowing the other to rest,
only seeing each other
for brief moments each day.

but the moon watches
the sun light up the sky,
and the sun watches
the moon control the tides,
and they are happy
because the other is
doing what they love.

life after you was freeing,
although that hurts to admit.
i was giving you all of me,
every ounce of my love,
and not getting a drop
in return.
i don't blame you for that—
for taking up the space that you did.

but when you were taking up all
of my space,
i was caged in a corner.
trapped in a mirror.
when i wasn't giving you
everything i had,
i prayed you would notice
me—
the way i grew
smaller and smaller to make room
for you.

i do not have smooth edges.
not on my body, face, mind.
i am made of sharp sides,
of chewed nails and picked skin.
my mind does not swim in gently flowing rivers—
it rages through riptides and dives below the dark.
it does not float through the wind like a petal,
no, it soars straight into the eye of a tornado,
spins sharply among the wreckage of its past.
my mind is not the smooth surface
of a carefully carved shell,
it is the rough edges of a cliff,
a step away from the fall.
there are no white-sand beaches here,
no barefoot walking.
you will feel stone and glass on your heels
with every step.

these walls are not a home,
just a shelter
to keep me warm.
and his arms were not a home,
just parts of a boy
who fooled me into feeling safe.

this body is my home.

and i don't always know
how to treat it that way,
but i'm trying.

i've never tasted poison, but i
imagine it tastes the way my
mouth felt after i said goodbye
to you.

i needed to let go
of you
so i could hold
on to me.

confessions: i sing in the shower and
dance when there's no music playing
and i say things i don't mean—
sometimes i regret it and
sometimes i don't.
now and then i'm selfish and sometimes
my back breaks from all the giving and
i don't know how to love myself
but i'm trying,
and i'm not that great at loving other people
but i'm trying.

the enchantment

love poems to myself and other reminders

i write poems often of love
for others.
about heartbreak
and romance
and happy endings.

but i've never written love poems
to myself.

today, that changes.

the first time i tried to write
a love poem to myself,
the page stayed blank.

i grabbed a pen and paper
and tried again the next day,
but still no words came.

on the third day, i sat
in front of my mirror
and smiled.

i noticed a dimple
just below my lips
on the right side of my chin

and i thought it was
beautiful. no poem i write
could capture

that moment—the first time
i looked in the mirror and saw
something worth writing about.

the next day,
i talked to my reflection
and i told her i loved her.
it was the first time i had ever
said it out loud.

i had never experienced something
so strange,
so glorious.

when you first left, i thought,
maybe if i had just
learned to love myself,
he would have stayed. but
i think if you really loved me,
you would have stayed
to watch me learn.

and here
i am,
learning.

i owe it to myself to
love me. not because
my body has carried
me through life and
held me up, but because
it has let me fall. it has
cried with me, felt pain
with me, and still lives
despite it all.

you are always so strong for others,
but have you forgotten that there is strength
in crumbling?
in allowing your eyes to water?
in relaxing your shoulders and bowing your head?

you are always so strong for others.
it's okay to be strong for yourself.

there is strength in saying goodbye
to the person you were so you can become
who you were meant to be.

there is strength in letting go.
unwrap your fingers from any hatred
you're carrying,
and show yourself forgiveness.

in my dreams,
i breathe fire,
burning everything in my path.
i step through piles of ash and never look back.

in my dreams,
i yell at the top of my lungs.
my voice echoes across valleys
and climbs up mountainsides.

and when i wake, i breathe lightly.
when i wake, i speak quietly.
when i wake, there is no fire.
is it wrong to wish for fire?

in another life
i walk proudly,
speak confidently,
wear what i want without
fearing others' eyes.
i dream sweetly,
make friends easily,
float through life without
a mistake.

in this life,
my voice shakes.
i don't like attention,
and i can be hard to talk to.
i have nightmares sometimes,
but i laugh often.
i think creatively and
i learn from my mistakes.

so today,
i'm really glad i'm in this life.

when i am alone, i talk to myself
and it is calming.
i take deep breaths and offer advice
and show myself love.
i say
your feelings are valid.
i say
it's okay to make mistakes.
i say
i am proud of you.

don't hide your happiness
with your hands.
let the world see how radiant you are
when you smile.

self-love exercises:

1. look at yourself in the mirror, pick three things you love about yourself and say them out loud.
2. think about something that makes you feel like your best self. make time for it each week.
3. write a love letter to yourself and keep it somewhere close. read it when you're feeling down.

i am not broken.
i am human.
and sometimes my pain
is visible
through bruises
and scrapes
and scars.
and sometimes my pain
is hidden,
carried deep within my heart.
there is a smile
on my face
and sadness inside.
but that does not mean
i am broken.
i am simply alive.

i get overwhelmed when i think about the future.
every time i open my eyes
i have no idea what could unfold,
so i admire the little things that
i know are here to stay,
like the sun peeking above the trees in the morning
and warm toes beneath my blanket as i fall asleep.
i listen to birds chirping hello in summer
and rain knocking on my window in spring,
breath turning to fog in winter
and leaves crunching beneath my feet in fall.
i melt chocolate on my tongue
and savor the taste.
there is so much beauty in this world,
and little time to waste.

to me in five years:

i hope when you look in the mirror, you smile.
i hope your voice doesn't still shake when
you speak but if it does, i hope you don't feel
ashamed to repeat what you said,
because your voice is powerful.

i really hope you know that you're valuable.

ask me to stay
and i'll stay.
tell me to go
and i'll go.
love me
and i will love you deeply.
break me and i

will pick up the pieces,
but i will not stay.

i will put myself back together,
but i will not stay.

i barely remember
the names and faces of the
people i
once tried
so hard to be.

my biggest mistake
was blaming my body
for being imperfect
instead of blaming
the ones who
made me
feel imperfect.

i wish i could tell my past self
that the person i'm meant to be
is not a cookie-cutter version
of everyone else. maybe i would
have stopped trying so hard to
shape my body into a mold that
never fit.

(i wish i could tell my past self
that it's a *good thing*
i didn't fit.)

my future self calls my name—
a soft, familiar voice echoing around me.
instinctively, my hands reach out
and she is there
folding hers over mine,
standing by my side.
she looks like me but stands taller,
chin held higher,
smile brighter.

i ask her what it's like where she is.
she says *it's beautiful.*

i ask what i can do to get there.
she says *you will.*

i hug her tightly. i wish i could melt
into her, become her.

i look down at my feet,
confess that i'm afraid.

chin up, she says. *there's so much ahead of you
that you won't want to miss.*

through the little things, people will tell you how much they care—checking in to make sure you got home safe. placing their coat around your shivering arms to keep you warm.

but people will show how little they care, too. here you are, fighting for their affection, putting them before you. tormenting yourself trying to figure out when they're going to change, when they're going to finally see you, while you've been standing right in front of them all along.

if they keep proving they don't value your time, thinking about them isn't worth your time.

loving someone will not
make you whole.
you are already whole.

my hands are cold
and for once, i am not
wishing for yours to hold.

i wonder if i will ever forget you
but for now, i am dreaming of
a worthy life without you.

for once, i am not thinking about
our ending—i am cherishing
my new beginning.

because even when i am alone,
i am with me.
the me that has so many dreams,

that never gives up,
that breathes into my hands
and creates my own warmth.

i thought i needed you then,
but now i know
i will never need you again.

you are worthy of so much more than someone
who doesn't reach for your hand when
you are down.

you are worthy of so much more than someone
who says they love you but whose actions
never show it.

you are worthy of so much more than someone
who expects you to change but does not
do any growing of their own.

you are worthy of someone who knows
what you're worth,
and never stops proving that to you.

when the right person
comes along and
loves you the way you deserve,
you will feel like floating.
not because they emptied you,
but because they raised you up.

and when it hurts like hell,
when the sadness buries you
in blankets and hides you
in heartache,
when your soul physically hurts—
painful throbs in your chest—
think about the healing.
with every tear that falls,
think about the healing.

time doesn't make everything
perfect, but it helps.
and though it feels awful,
like you can't imagine a day
where the pain doesn't hang
heavy around your ankles,
i promise, a day will come when
the heaviness feels a little lighter.

i'll be okay and so will you.
i'm still alive and so are you.
sometimes we fall and that's okay.
bravely we fight for one more day.

don't listen to anyone
who tells you
never look back.
self-growth
is one of the most
important reminders we have.

to look back at who you
were and see how
much you've grown.
how beautiful it is to
love who you are
and never feel alone.

girl made of glass

to my teenage self:

i want to tell you that we
no longer look in the mirror and
wish we could shatter.
i want to tell you that there
are bad days but we are whole.

we are happy.

i want to tell you that it
gets so much better.

i want to thank you for
never giving up.

when i was young,
i wished i could be
anyone but me.

now that i've changed
myself, i'm searching for
the girl i used to be.

she vanished before
my eyes. i pray she's
not gone for good.

but i promise
if she comes back,
i will love her like i should.

i'm learning to be okay with slow growth—
with gentle steps instead of giant leaps.
i see others ahead of me and behind me,
but i know i am where i need to be.

we spend so much time searching
for our past selves, but
what if they aren't meant to be found?
what if we are exactly who we're supposed to be?
what if we've grown so much
that we wouldn't recognize our past selves anyway?

i am welcoming myself
back with open arms,
loving myself
with a full heart.

if you don't know
where to begin,
forgiving yourself is
a beautiful start.

acknowledgments

thank you to my parents for instilling in me a fierce determination to work hard and never give up. and for driving me to the library many, *many* times as a kid.

thank you to michelle, my publisher, for giving this book a welcoming home.

thank you to my agent, james, for helping me find this book a home.

thank you to my readers for bringing my words into your hearts. thank you for making me feel less alone.

thank you to my partner, simon, for being endlessly supportive of everything i do.

about shelby leigh

shelby leigh is an author who explores mental health, self-love, and healing through poetry. she is the author of *changing with the tides* and *it starts like this*. she wrote her third and newest collection, *girl made of glass*, to examine the past and how it can haunt our minds through overthinking. she writes her books with the goal of making others feel less alone and empowering her readers to love who they are. when leigh isn't writing, you can find her reading a good book, buying yellow decor, and/or probably eating chocolate.

keep up with her at @shelbyleighpoetry or shelbyleigh.co

more great poetry from central avenue publishing

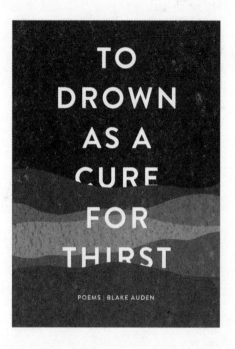

To Drown as a Cure for Thirst is a delicate exploration of grief, and how it affects — and is affected by — time and memory.

Written in the wake of a global pandemic, the book touches on themes including loss, healing, personal reflection, mental health, and love, even in the face of the things that haunt us. Auden's most personal and deeply honest collection to date, these pages examine the idea that we can overcome what winter has taken, and that to hurt is simply an act of remembering.

the

surrender

theory

poems

Caitlin Conlon

The Surrender Theory begins in the thick of heartbreak, gets lost in the vibrancy of new love, and eventually rediscovers itself in a place of peace and closure. It's about learning to grow alongside grief. About taking the hand of your younger self and forgiving them. Through pages of truisms and poems, this debut collection from Caitlin Conlon explores the boundaries of our most poignant and human emotions.

Deeply personal yet universal, *The Surrender Theory* speaks to anyone who has put their heart out into the world and hoped with everything in them that it would come home unscathed.

i gave myself the world showcases the beauty
of introspection and exploring personal
conflict. Through a conversation with an
inner voice, Catarine Hancock portrays and
symbolizes the peaks, valleys, and plateaus
of the journey toward recognizing self-
worth. This collection of uplifting verse is a
balm for the soul in need of peace and will
help the reader grow into the person they're
meant to be.